101 Ways to Survive

FOUR MORE YEARS!!

of

George W. Bush.

by Pat Bagley

101 Ways to Survive Four More Years of
George W. Bush
copyright 2005   Pat Bagley
all rights reserved
Printed in the United States

editor: Dan Thomas

First Edition

9 8 7 6 5 4 3 2

No portion of this book may be reproduced in any form with-
out the express written permission from the publisher,
White Horse Books, 1347 S. Glenmare St.
Salt Lake City, Utah 84105
ISBN 0-9744860-4-3

White Horse Books 1347 S. Glenmare St.
Salt Lake City, UT 84105 (801) 556-4615
www.utahwhitehorsebooks.com

101 Ways to Survive Four More Years of George W. Bush

by Pat Bagley

1.

Go live
in a
cave.

You won't miss much. You can have somebody tape "The Simpsons" for you.

2.

Write a
children's
book.

"Curious George Goes to War."

3.

Find the Democratic party.

4.

Get
in
shape.

Burn off those unwanted pounds while working out that sense of powerless frustration.

5.

Scrapbook
the end of
the world.

Keeping one's hands busy is a terrific way to deal with anxiety.

6.

Find
personal peace
through faith.

7.

Move to Australia.

CRIKEY, MATE!
YOUR PRESIDENT HAS A FEW KANGAROOS LOOSE IN THE UPPER PADDOCK!

8.

Shop.

Someone's got to keep those loose nukes on ebay out of the hands of terrorists.

9.

Go on an extended vacation.

Even snotty French waiters
will feel sorry for you.

10.

Apologize
to the
whole
world.

I'M SORRY MY PRESIDENT IS AN IDIOT.

11.

Hug
a
tree.

Then kiss it goodbye.

12.

Move
to a
blue state.

Never mind, you probably already
live in one.

13.

Take up
fortune
telling.

It will be surprisingly easy for the next four years.

14.

Open a travel agency for Republicans.

Send them to all those wonderful and happy places in Iraq the media isn't showing them.

15.

Defend the Constitution with your life.

Plenty of Bush supporters will defend it with your life as well.

16.

Go
#@%*!
yourself.

You may have to take a number.

17.

Don't be too happy when you find out Bush has an intern problem.

LIBERALS INTERNED IN BIBLE CAMPS
BUSH SAYS "FAITH MAKES FREE"

18.

Act presidential.
Say inspiring stuff
while strutting around
in a flight suit.

Funny how when you do it, it suddenly sounds like lunatic babble.

19.

Start an
office
pool.

Bet on the next country we'll invade.

20.

Hope Bush appoints better foreign policy advisors.

Suddenly all those Miss Americas look a lot more attractive.

21.

Join the Bush
Cultural
Revolution.

"The Wisdom of George Bush" is a very short read.

22.

Enlist.
Heroically
serve your
country in
Iraq.

When you come back and run for office as an anti-war candidate, GOP political operatives will question your patriotism.

23.

Get drunk
with Colin
Powell.

Find out the real poop.

24.

Get over it.

Send your president a gift to show
there are no hard feelings.

25.

Swap Bush
with a
trained
monkey.

It will be at least six weeks before anyone notices.

26.

Gloat when
things go bad.

It will be a small, but satisfying pleasure.

27.

Slip truth serum into Limbaugh's oxycontin.

28.

Take up a
collection to
buy Congress
a spine.

29.

Throw caution
to the wind.

You've always wanted to travel.

30.

Make every
room in your
house a panic
room.

31.

Lobby the U.N. for
election monitors
in 2008.

32.

When life hands you a lemon . . .

. . . make lemonade.

33.

Use the
"Bush method"
to motivate
your child.

34.

Get away
from it all.
Go fishing.

YA KNOW, IT REALLY CHAPS MY GILLS THE WAY BUSH IS TURNING MY POND INTO A TOILET.

35.

Sign up for
the Bush
Health Plan.

36.

Find a deserted island.

When you're ready to be rescued, you can vote yourself off in 2008.

37.

Ghost write
Bush's
political
autobiography.

38.

Put everything
in Halliburton
stock.

You'll begin to see things differently.

39.

Lying means never having to say you're sorry.

NOPE.
CAN'T THINK OF ANYTHING I'VE DONE WRONG...
ABU GHRAIB
BRING IT ON
OSAMA
WMDs
IRAQ
9-11 COMMIS
PLAME SCANDAL
MISSION ACCOMPLISHED
SMEAR TACTICS
WAR

40.

Rescue an abused animal.

The Oval Office parrot comes to mind.

41.

See no Bush.
Hear no Bush.
Speak no Bush.

Cancel your paper. Turn off the news.
Avoid your friends.

42.

Whatever
doesn't kill
you makes
you stronger.

When the time comes, you'll be very, very strong.

43.

Engage in a favorite neo-conservative pastime.

Like pulling the wings off flies.

44.

Call
conservative
talk shows.

But only if you're into abuse.

45.

Time to take
the magic bus
down off the
cinder blocks.

And dust off those anti-establishment slogans that are suddenly back in style.

46.

Move to
Canada.

You'll have plenty of company.

47.

Move
somewhere
warm.

Like Canada. (By the way, there is no such thing as global warming—no matter how many scientific studies Bush has to suppress).

48.

You can't fool
all the people
all the time.

A simple majority will do.

49.

Enter anger
management.

TVs can get expensive.

50.

Beware
of blog.

Resist the urge to share your post-election angst in excruciating detail on the web. Please.

51.

Prove the
election
was stolen.

Denial is not just a river in Egypt.

52.

Crawl into
the bottle.

You can sober up in four years
and run for president.

53.

Let our
troops in
harm's way
know you
care.

The people who put them there
are too busy with world domination
to bother.

54.

Make the
president's
new clothes.

There's nothing to it.

55.

Beg Agent
Smith to
reinsert you
into the
Matrix.

56.

Consider where others are coming from.

They may not know your feelings about Bush.

57.

Count your
blessings.

Things could be worse.

58.

Don't drill
holes in your
head.

The pressure in your skull when you think about Bush is, well, all in your head. It really won't explode.

59.

Take a farewell
tour of America's
national parks.

60.

Find a creative
outlet to
express your
disappointment.

61.

Outsource Bush
to something
he's good at.

62.

Love your
country.

Bush is a temporary condition.
America is greater than a pious twerp
with delusions of grandeur.

63.

Play the home
version of
"Fear Factor."

64.

Fight the Right.

Liberals can play the fear card, too.

65.

Just, ya know,
trust in the
president.

Britney Spears: the intellectual architect of the Bush administration.

66.

Plan ahead for
a comfortable
retirement.

67.

Rat out those
you suspect of
being evildoers
and haters of
freedom.

Like your boss!

68.

Ignorance
is bliss.

It's also the fast track to advancement in the Bush administration.

69.

Enjoy your
new drug
benefit
program.

70.

Spend like a
drunken
sailor.

A. It's good for the economy.
B. Jesus will come before
   the bill is due.

71.

Get off your donkey and get with the program!

Trade in your pansy-assed liberalism for red-meat values and red-state accessories.

72.

Live the
American
Dream.

Get born to a U.S. president who has wealthy friends.

73.

Simplify
your taxes.

Cut out the IRS middle man. Send your taxes straight to a defense contractor.

74.

Be
positive.

Toadies and Yes Men are in demand these days.

75.

Wear
black.

Mourning in America.

76.

Try the Rip
van Winkle
gambit.

Fall asleep for twenty years and wake up to an America without King George.

77.

They lie,
we lie.

78.

Don't sweat
the small
stuff.

Sweat the big stuff.

79.

Rest easy.

Team Bush will keep you safe.

80.

Take a sabbatical.

Your brain needs a break from
Bush-bashing books.

81.

Stuff White House fortune cookies.

YOU WILL NOT DO ANOTHER WAR TODAY.
GOOD FORTUNE COMES YOUR WAY AFTER RESIGNING.
YOUR DAUGHTERS ARE DATING MICHAEL MOORE.
ANNOUNCE TO THE WORLD YOUR DIVINITY!
THE HAVES AND HAVE-MORES HAVE ENOUGH.
THE NEW INTERN THINKS YOURE HOT!
KARL ROVE IS PLOTTING A COUP!

82.

Get the
ultimate in
homeland
security.

Your food storage consists of enough
ammo to seize your neighbor's.

83.

Figure out why Democrats didn't run a candidate with more appeal than Bush.

Like a dead cat.

84.

Go to
Mars.

It's only called the Red Planet. That doesn't mean it voted Republican.

85.

Play a
name game.

Bush likes to give people clever pet names, like Stinky, Brainy, or Smarty. Give him one, too. Here are a few suggestions:

DUMBYA

BLUNDER BUSH

SAGE of CRAWFORD

THE GREAT UNITER

DUMB AND DUBYA

SKIP (RE: NATIONAL GUARD) SERVICE

GOD'S GUNSLINGER

OUR FEARLESS LEADER

YOUR OWN PET NAME FOR BUSH HERE ↗

86.

Don't worry,
be happy.

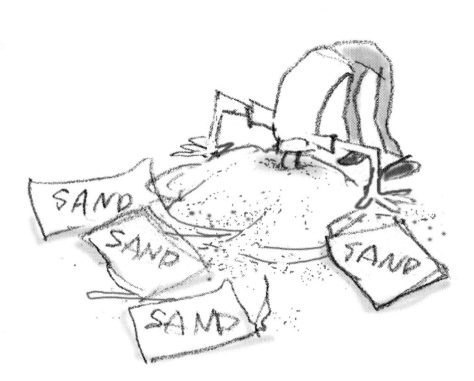

87.

Ease
human
suffering.

Invent a device that masks the sound of Bush.

88.

Got
morals?

Getting weepy over a clump of cells
shows you have high moral values.

89.

Help Bush
remember.

He can't think of a single mistake he's made? Early alzheimer's?

- [ ] SURPLUS TO DEFICIT
- [ ] WMDS
- [ ] IRAQ CAKE WALK
- [ ] PLAME SCANDAL
- [ ] OSAMA
- [ ] 9-11
- [ ] OPPOSING CREATION OF 9-11 COMMISSION
- [ ] 9-11, IRAQ LINK
- [ ] DIRTY SMEAR CAMPAIGN
- [ ] FOULING WATER AND AIR

- [ ] TRASHING BILL OF RIGHTS
- [ ] ABU GHRAIB
- [ ] INSUFFICIENT TROOPS
- [ ] INTELLIGENCE FAILURE
- [ ] NUCLEAR N. KOREA
- [ ] DISAPPEARING WORLD LEADERSHIP
- [ ] CHALABI
- [ ] DIVIDED NATION
- [ ] SELLING AMERICA CHEAP TO CORPORATIONS
- [ ] _____

USE EXTRA PAGES FOR 2ND TERM

90.

Learn an
exotic foreign
language.

The government needs translators.

91.

Give Bush
credit for his
Clear Skies
initiative.

Bye, bye, birdie.

92.

Patent a B.S.
detector.

93.

Americans must have a reason for re-electing Bush.

It doesn't necessarily have to be a good one.

WINKY AND TUFFY
LIKED KERRY, BUT
SAUCY, PRINCESS, KIP
AND CRUMPET LIKED
THE PRESIDENT'S
"NO KITTY LEFT
BEHIND" PROGRAM.

94.

Find that
special
someone.

All you need is love.

ILOATHEBUSH.COM
SOULMATCH

bummed4now   PROFILE

TURN ONS: LISTENING TO NPR.
RANTS ABOUT BUSH

TURN OFFS: NEO-CONS, WORLD
DOMINATION

MORE PHOTOS

ABOUT ME:
I WAS RECENTLY HURT BY
A DISAPPOINTING PRESIDEN-
TIAL CANDIDATE. BUT MY
HEART IS OPEN TO BEING
WITH SOMEONE WHO IS
SMART, PASSIONATE, GEN-
UINE, AND AGAINST THE
WAR IN IRAQ.

FAVORITE
BOOKS: "BUSHWHACKED"
"BUSH IS WRECKING
EVERYTHING."
"BUSH IS A CON-
GENITAL IDIOT"
"DUBYA DUBYA III"
"BUSH: ALIEN
ABDUCTEE?"
"BUSH; OH MY GOD!"

95.

Thou shalt not be a religious ignoramus.

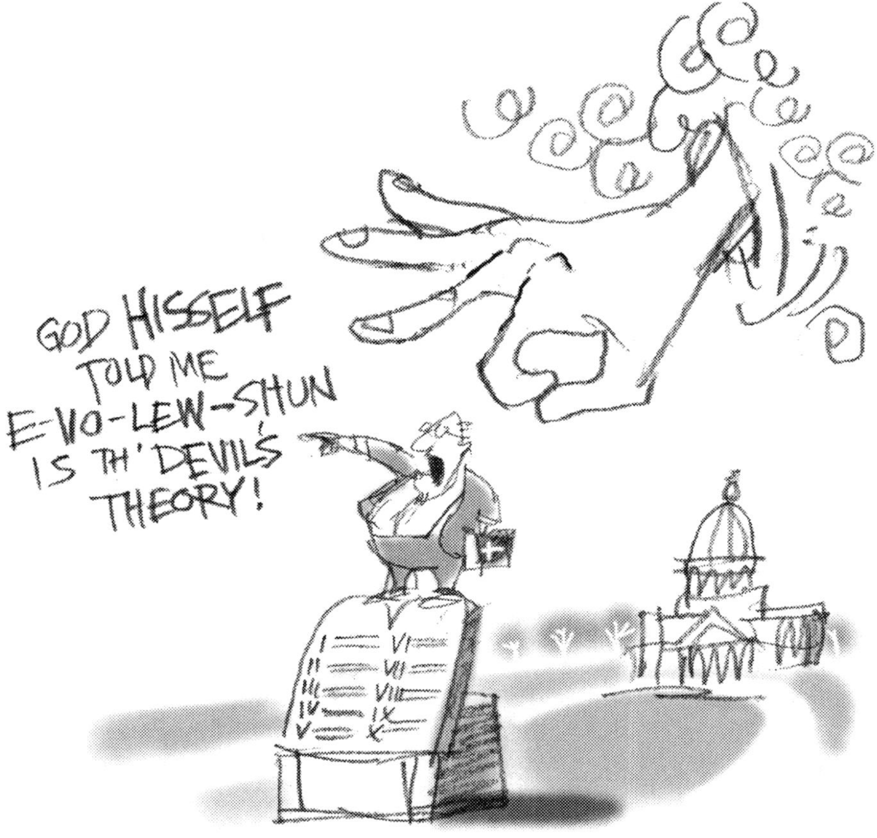
GOD HISSELF TOLD ME E-VO-LEW-SHUN IS TH' DEVIL'S THEORY!

96.

Take a deep
breath.

Now, slooowly let it out. Good. Breath in. Out. In. Out . . . Just 37,426,278 more and he'll be gone.

97.

Grab a flight
somewhere.

You can worry where later.

98.

Try new
culinary
treats.

·Half-baked Texas Turkey
·Hot-buttered Rumsfeld
·Cheney Dipped in Oil
  and, of course . . .
·Condoleezza Rice

99.

Meditate.
Empty your
mind . . .

Not that empty!

100.

Don't
despair.

The Constitution says he can't
run again.

101.

Wake up!

There's still a chance it's all just a horrible dream.

For Alec and Buzz
and a better tomorrow.